We Can Do Hard Things

A Story of a Mother's Journey with Breast Cancer through the Eyes of Her Daughter

Written by Melissa Dupuis
Illustrated by Maddy Moore

Briley & Baxter Publications | Plymouth, Massachusetts

Hardcover ISBN: 978-1-961978-60-7
Paperback ISBN: 978-1-961978-61-4

Book Design: Stacy O'Halloran

This book is dedicated to my daughter, Sage. Thank you for keeping me present through the biggest fight of my life. I love you baby girl—to the stars, all the way to my toes!

One day, Mama had to go to the hospital because she was sick. She was really scared, and I was too, but she told me that we can be brave and do hard things together.

While she was at the hospital, I drew her a picture of us to show her that we're a team and that we can do hard things together.

Mama said it wasn't anyone's fault she was sick, and it was okay for me to have feelings about it. She seemed sad, and I was sad, too.

Mama seemed to love it whenever I wrapped my arms around her and squeezed her tight. Our hugs made me feel better, too!

I asked her if her sickness was something I could catch, like a cold. She said it was a different kind of illness—something I couldn't catch—so the best thing I could do for her was give her extra love and hugs. I have always loved giving her hugs and kisses, so that part was not hard for me!

Mama said she was feeling scared but strong and that I should share my feelings, too, because we can be brave together.

Sometimes drawing pictures helped me describe how I was feeling.

Mama had to take medication to make her sickness go away. She didn't like it, but she knew it would help her feel better. I could relate because sometimes I had to take medicine when I was sick, and I didn't like it either—but, as Mama said, we can do hard things together.

Some days, Mama didn't have the energy to play with me like she used to before she got sick, but that didn't mean she didn't love me. We found other ways to play together, like reading books and doing puzzles! Puzzles could be hard for me, just like being sick was hard on Mama, but we did hard things together.

On most days, Mama went to the hospital while I was at school. I gave her one of my stuffies to bring to the hospital and help her feel brave. I brought another stuffy to school and hugged it while thinking of her.

One day, I asked Mama why she didn't have hair anymore. It was hard for me to see her look so different. She said the medicine made her lose her hair, but it would grow back. It was hard for her to lose her hair.

To cheer her up, we decided to have some fun and try on different hats to keep her head warm. It was like playing dress-up! I wondered what her hair would look like when it grew back. I liked rubbing her head; it felt soft, and it made her happy when I kissed it.

Mama always encouraged me to ask questions. It was hard for me to understand what she was going through, and it was hard for her to answer all of my questions. But, we knew we were a team and that we can do hard things together.

Mama said it was important to take care of our bodies, so she made sure we both ate nutritious foods. Sometimes that was hard for her because she didn't feel well, so I made her soup. She gobbled it up because it was made with my special ingredient—love!

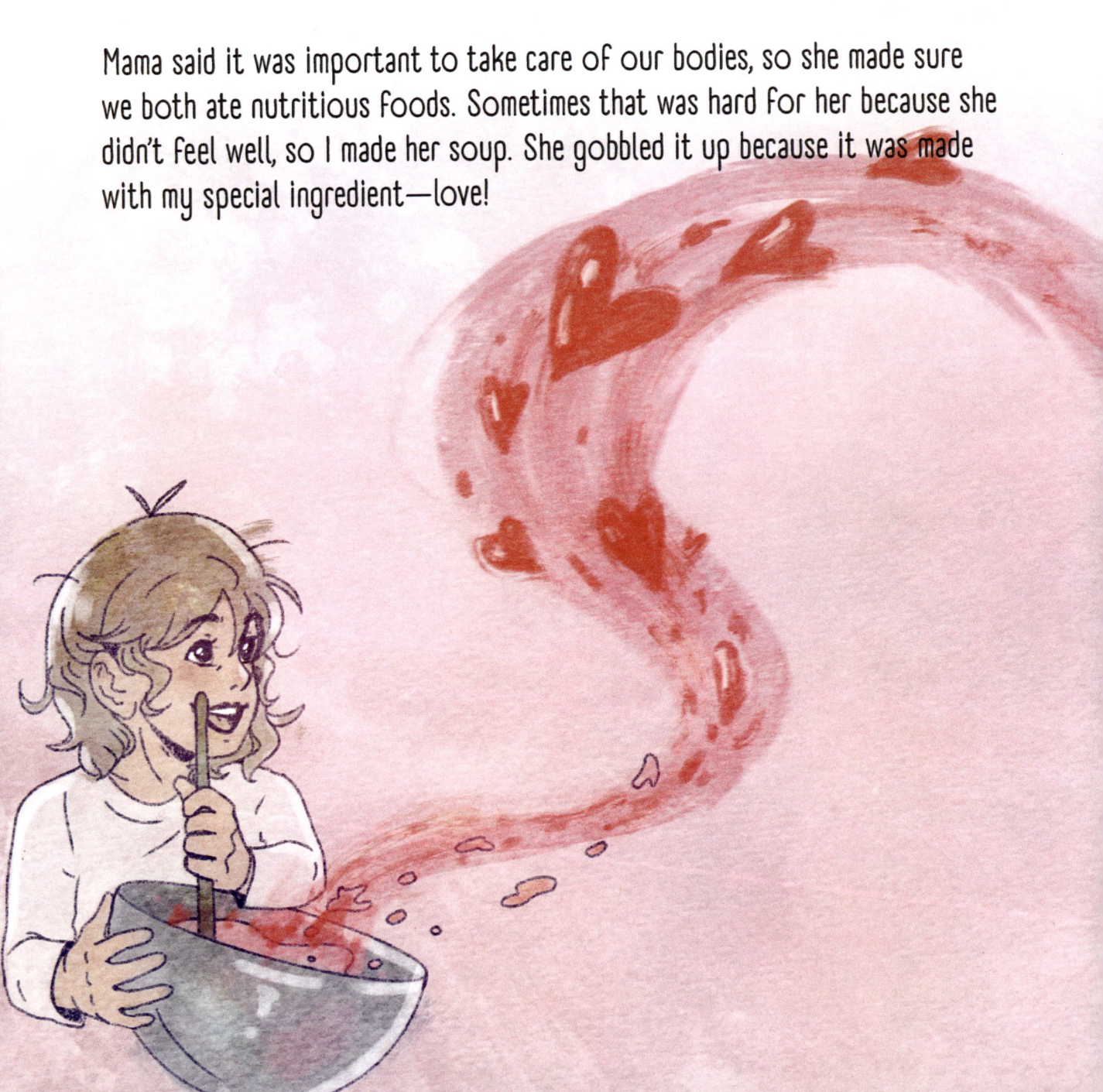

To stay healthy, Mama and I exercised together. It was hard for Mama to exercise because she was tired. Some of the moves were hard for me, too, but we did it together and had fun!

Dancing was my favorite form of exercise, so when Mama was feeling up for it, we would have dance parties! It always made us laugh and smile.

Through Mama's sickness, she taught me that life is a gift—like a present you get on your birthday—so each day is special.

Mama is healthy now, and we are both so happy!

When Mama was sick, we faced a lot of hard things, but we overcame them together. I know we can do hard things, and guess what?

About the Author

Melissa, a first-time author, is so grateful to be able to bring her story to life! She was born in Massachusetts and grew up as a professional ballet dancer in the Boston area. She currently teaches pilates in Boston and on the North Shore. As a health and wellness advocate, she lives and breathes a healthy lifestyle for herself, her family, and her clients. Therefore, when she was diagnosed with Stage three HER2+ breast cancer at the age of thirty-eight, her world was rocked. She couldn't believe a healthy person such as herself could get so sick. She was a new mom of a beautiful baby girl, who was just one year old at the time. Throughout her year of treatment (chemo, double mastectomy, and radiation), she maintained her healthy lifestyle as best as she could, striving to show her daughter her strength and to set an example for women everywhere to be advocates for their own health. She was inspired to write this story of her journey through her daughter's eyes as a way to give back to the cancer community. This story is a way for others to share their diagnosis with their young children and show them that, no matter what life throws at you, you can do hard things. Whether it's a cancer diagnosis or tying your shoes, your little ones will be inspired to keep trying, be strong, and do the hard things!

She resides in the North Shore with her beautiful family: her husband, daughter Sage, son Asher, and Australian Shepherd Stanlee. After treatment, she got back on the stage to perform the Nutcracker and is so grateful that she is healthy and happy. Never take life for granted—it's truly a gift!

Note from the Author

I want to thank my husband for being my rock during this journey, my family for constantly being there, my friends that are my family, and my cancer community that got me through this. I am beyond grateful for my two miracle children who inspire me every day to be my best self. I am so thankful to share this story of strength and courage through my daughter's eyes.

About the Illustrator

Maddy is a professional illustrator who has been working in the industry for well over a decade. Maddy grew up in an international family and has consequently lived and worked in various corners of the world. She began her career as an artist at fifteen, where she would complete commission-based illustrations around her commitments as she pursued her Bachelor of Arts at the University of Pennsylvania. Maddy's art can be viewed at: maddymoore.art.

www.ingramcontent.com/pod-product-compliance
Lightning Source LLC
Chambersburg PA
CBRC090831120626
46547CB00008B/656